GW00854547

ENJOYING CHRIST

AS THE
ALL-INCLUSIVE

SPIRIT

FOR THE PRACTICAL,
GENUINE, AND REAL

CHURCH LIFE

WITNESS LEE

Living Stream Ministry

Anaheim, CA · www.lsm.org

First Edition, September 2009.

ISBN 978-0-7363-4207-0

Published by

Living Stream Ministry
2431 W. La Palma Ave., Anaheim, CA 92801 U.S.A.
P. O. Box 2121, Anaheim, CA 92814 U.S.A.

Printed in the United States of America

09 10 11 12 13 14 15 / 9 8 7 6 5 4 3 2 1

CONTENTS

PREFACE

The following are messages given by Brother Witness Lee in San Francisco, California, from December 29, 1972 to January 1, 1973.

CHAPTER ONE

BEING SAVED FROM THE PRESENT EVIL AGE BY GOD REVEALING HIS SON IN US

Scripture Reading: Gal. 1:1-4, 6-7, 10-16, 22-23

The entire Bible is a revelation from God, breathed out by Him (2 Tim. 3:16; 2 Pet. 1:20-21), and the order of the books of the Bible is also sovereignly arranged by God. We cannot put Genesis at the end of the Bible, put Revelation at the beginning, or rearrange the Gospels and Acts. Rather, all the books in the Bible are in a proper sequence. In the New Testament we first have the four Gospels, presenting a full picture of a wonderful person, the Lord Jesus Christ. Following this is Acts, with the preaching, propagating, ministering, and imparting of this wonderful One into many persons. After Peter's first preaching, about three thousand people were saved, and later another five thousand believed (2:41; 4:4). Eventually, many people believed in Jesus and received Him into them. In the four Gospels Christ was an individual person, but after being imparted into many people in Acts, this Christ is now in many thousands of believers.

Now what God wants to do with these believers is to bring them together. We Christians can be compared to bees. Bees do not care to be individualistic; they prefer to be corporate. It is difficult to find a bee altogether by itself, because bees always tend to gather together. It is not that they are forced to be together; rather, this is the tendency of their nature. Moreover, when bees are collected together, they lose their identity. It is difficult to identify individual bees in a hive. Butterflies, on the other hand, often behave individually and not in large groups, and their individual beauty stands out for a display. People appreciate the beauty of a butterfly, but bees are not recognized for their individual beauty. This is a good illustration of Christians. We Christians are like bees, not butterflies. We forget about cultivating individualistic beauty in a peculiar way and simply gather together in a corporate way. This corporate life and work are revealed in the book of Acts.

Following Acts is the first Epistle, the book of Romans. Although many would say that Romans is a book on justification by faith, justification is only the beginning, not the goal. The final subject in Romans is the Body of Christ. Chapter 12 begins, "I exhort you therefore, brothers, through the compassions of God to present your bodies a living sacrifice...that you may prove what the will of God is" (vv. 1-2). This is the will of God not in a general way but in a very specific way. According to this chapter, the particular will of God is to have the Body life (vv. 4-5). This is the consummating revelation in the book of Romans.

Now all the believers who have the life of God in them are a corporate people, because the divine life within them is a collective, corporate life. Deep within every Christian is the desire to "flock" together. A common proverb says, "Birds of a feather flock together." In actuality, it is not having the same feathers that brings birds together; it is having the same life within them. Because we all have Christ as the same life within us (Col. 3:4), we gather together as the Body. It is difficult to enjoy the Lord by ourselves as much as we do in the meetings of the church. This is because we have a corporate life within us, which is Christ Himself. We all have a deep desire to be together with the other saints. This is according to the disposition of the spiritual life within us, which is Christ. This togetherness is the best communal and social life. I have been "social" in this way for many years. Everywhere I travel, I meet many seekers of Jesus. Out of this spiritual disposition that desires to flock together, the Body is produced.

Although coming together as the Body is wonderful, sometimes certain problems result. Therefore, after Romans comes 1 Corinthians, which shows us the way to deal with the problems. These problems come mainly from two sources. The first source is dead, doctrinal knowledge. The more dead knowledge we have, the more problems there are. The second source of problems is the improper practice of the gifts. Many problems issued from the knowledge and gifts of the Corinthians. Paul tells them, "Knowledge puffs up, but love builds up" (8:1). The divisions that the Corinthians suffered came from their differing kinds of knowledge and practice of the gifts (1:10-12; 12:18-22, 25, 28-30). In contrast to this, Paul says that we were all given to drink one Spirit (v. 13). The best way to solve all the problems is to drink Jesus, who is the Spirit today.

First Corinthians 15:45b says, "The last Adam became a life-giving Spirit." Some say that it is heresy to teach that Jesus is the Spirit. However, if the life-giving Spirit, whom Christ became, is not the Holy Spirit, what Spirit is He? We do not believe that there is another life-giving Spirit besides the Holy Spirit. To say this is a real heresy. We believe in the Divine Trinity in the way of the Bible, not in the way of tradition. The traditional teaching of the Trinity gives people the impression that there are three Gods—the Father is one God, the Son is another, and the Spirit is yet another. Rather, there is only one God (8:4). In 1 Corinthians we are told that Christ as the last Adam became the life-giving Spirit, and we have been given to drink of this one Spirit. The way to solve the problems in the church is not to gain more dead knowledge or to have more practice of the gifts. It is to drink of Christ as the life-giving Spirit by calling "Lord Jesus" (12:3b). This causes us to be one.

Following this Epistle is 2 Corinthians, which tells us that Jesus as the life-giving Spirit is the indwelling and transforming One, whom we must behold and reflect with an unveiled face (3:17-18). However, 2 Corinthians does not tell us in detail what the veils are.

GALATIANS DEALING WITH THE VEIL OF RELIGION

In order to know the subjective, indwelling, and transforming Jesus, we need to see more concerning the veils. To this end, following 2 Corinthians there is the book of Galatians. Strictly speaking, sin is not a veil that covers people, because everyone knows that sin is evil. Likewise, the world does not veil us, because many who seek God know that the world also is evil. The primary veil revealed in Galatians is religion. In the eyes of many people, religion is a good thing. No dictionary or lexicon tells us that religion is something negative. Apparently, religion causes people to be for God, to fear Him, and to worship Him. In actuality, religion is the strongest, thickest veil.

The first layer of covering that veils our eyes is religion, and the second layer is tradition. In every religion there are many traditions. Before Saul was saved, he was not worldly or sinful; he was altogether religious and traditional. He says, "I advanced in Judaism beyond many contemporaries in my race, being more abundantly a zealot for the traditions of my fathers" (1:14). He was a model of a topmost religious person, outranking others and excelling in religion and tradition. Nevertheless, he was blinded by his veils from seeing Christ, God's will, and the church (cf. Acts 9:8; Phil. 3:4-8). Saul's veils were the typical, sound, biblical religion of Judaism along with its many traditions.

Saul was not for the world or for anything sinful. He considered that he was fully for God, but blinded by the veils of religion and tradition, he persecuted the churches excessively and ravaged them (Gal. 1:13). One day he went to the high priest to receive the authority to bind the members of the church, all those who call on the name of Jesus. While Saul was on the way to Damascus, the Lord Jesus appeared and shined on him, and he was knocked down. The Lord said, "Saul, Saul, why are you persecuting Me?" (Acts 9:4). Saul was surprised, thinking that he had never persecuted anyone in the heavens. All the ones whom he had persecuted were the disciples on the earth. Saul asked, "Who are You, Lord?" When he called, "Lord," Jesus came into him. Then Jesus said, "I am Jesus, whom you persecute" (v. 5). At this point Saul lost his sight. One who says he is confident that he can see indicates that he is actually blind, but one who confesses that he is spiritually blind is in the position to receive revelation. Many religious people say, "I know there is one God. I know the sixty-six books of the Bible. In fact, I know many things."

Much of their knowledge, however, is of a religious and traditional nature, becoming veils to cover their sight. We need the Lord to come and take away all the veils so that we may gain inward sight and revelation.

SATAN UTILIZING RELIGION TO KEEP PEOPLE FROM CHRIST AND THE CHURCH AS GOD'S WILL

Nothing used by Satan is as subtle as religion. Satan uses sin and worldliness to keep people from God, but it is easy to understand that sin and the world are not good. However, it is difficult to realize that religion is a strong enemy of Christ. Satan utilizes the veil of religion to deceive people. This is true not only of Judaism but even of Christianity, which is a more developed religion. We may compare Satan's system to a large university, in which there are many departments. In Satan's "university" there are departments of dancing and drinking for those who like those things, but if someone considers those things to be ungodly, Satan will offer them a better department—the department of religion. Because the people in this department kneel, pray, fear God, and praise Him, it seems very attractive.

As long as Satan can keep someone away from Christ and His Body as the will of God, he is satisfied. However, there is no "department" of the genuine church in Satan's system. The Lord said, "I will build My church, and the gates of Hades shall not prevail against it" (Matt. 16:18). Satan is truly afraid of the church. If someone seeks after dead and doctrinal knowledge, he can find it in Satan's department of religion, but if some proclaim themselves in a proper way to be the church, Satan trembles. Many good Christians today have been cheated by Satan. They may speak about the Body of Christ, but they have no practice of the Body. They may even say, "It is too difficult to have the church life. Once you touch the matter of the church, you have many problems. It is wiser to stay away from it." This is the subtlety of the enemy. The wonderful Jesus has been imparted into the believers for the purpose of the Body and the practical church life. We must not expect that some day in the future the church will arrive or that the church will be in heaven. Rather, the church must be here today on the earth, even in our own locality. If we are not in the church life, we are still veiled and are being cheated.

CHRIST, THE CHURCH, GOD, AND REVELATION BEING VERSUS RELIGION, TRADITION, MAN, AND THE TEACHING OF MAN

In Galatians 1 there are four negative items and four positive ones. On the negative side there are religion (represented by Judaism—vv. 13-14), tradition (v. 14), man (vv. 1, 11-12), and the teaching of man (v. 12). Then on the positive side we have Christ, who is versus religion (vv. 1, 12, 16); the church, which is versus tradition (v. 13); God, who is versus man (vv. 10, 15); and revelation, which is versus the teaching of man (vv. 12, 16). Paul was "an apostle (not from men nor through man but through Jesus Christ and God the Father, who raised Him from the dead)" (v. 1). Paul's source and origin as an apostle was not man but God. Moreover, the gospel he announced to the Galatians was not according to man, received from man, nor taught by man (vv. 11-12). Rather, his gospel was received through a revelation of Jesus Christ. Teaching produces a religion, in which there are many traditions, but a revelation conveys and imparts Christ, issuing in the church, which is God's will. God, Christ, the church, and revelation are versus man, religion, tradition, and the teaching of man.

RELIGION BEING THE PRESENT EVIL AGE

Verse 4 says, "Who gave Himself for our sins that He might rescue us out of the present evil age." Paul's emphasis here is not that we are rescued from hell but that we are rescued out of the present age. The world as a whole is Satan's system, which is divided into many different ages. The nineteenth century was one age, and the twentieth century is another. Before World War I was one age, and after World War II was another. The 1960s brought yet another age with a certain kind of behavior, dress, and appearance. All these ages put together compose the world. Paul says that Christ gave Himself for our sins to rescue us out of the present evil age. According to the context of Galatians, the present age at

Paul's time was religion. To be rescued from religion at that time was to be delivered from the present evil age.

At the time of the apostle Paul, Judaism had become the "modern" religion in the regions of the Mediterranean Sea, including Asia Minor, where Galatia was. To be one who was circumcised, who kept the Sabbath, and who kept the ordinances concerning eating according to Leviticus was to be an up-to-date religious person. In the same principle today, Christianity is the modern, popular religion of much of the world. To be modern is simply to be according to the present age. Thus, to be delivered out of the present evil age is to be delivered out of something modern. Christ gave Himself for our sins that He might deliver us out of the religion of the modern age, which in Paul's time was the religion of Judaism and in our own time is the religion of Christianity.

A dictionary may tell us that *religion* is a good word, but Galatians 1 indicates that religion is versus Christ. It is something that persecutes the church, ravages it, and tries to root it out. Some may say that Judaism is the wrong religion, and now we have the right religion. However, this is not accurate. Religion is anything done for Christ but not having the presence and reality of Christ. Judaism was a religion founded according to the holy Word, just as today the fundamental things of Christianity are also based on the Word of God. Nevertheless, many in Christianity honor only its outward traditions and holidays without being truly for Christ in a pure way. By this we can see that religion is versus Christ. Today we still need to be delivered from the present evil age of religion.

In God's eyes, the old and traditional practices in Christianity without the presence and reality of Christ are a part of the present evil age. The religious age is evil because it keeps people from Christ and the church as God's will. There is nothing as evil in God's eyes as that which keeps us from Christ. In this principle, traditional and religious Christianity today is the present evil age, just as Judaism was in the days of the apostles. At that time, it was not mainly the world or the sinners that opposed the apostles. It was Judaism as the present evil age. The Jewish religion even condemned the

Lord Jesus to death according to their understanding of the Scriptures. Paul says, "You have heard of my manner of life formerly in Judaism, that I persecuted the church of God excessively and ravaged it" (v. 13). Is this not evil? What can be more evil than this? Man discerns religion according to the view of tradition and morality, but God discerns it from the view of His eternal purpose. Nothing damages God's eternal purpose as much as religion. Millions of people have been distracted by Catholicism and the Christian denominations. On the one hand, they bring people to God initially, but on the other hand, they distract people from God's eternal purpose to have the church as the built-up Body of Christ in oneness. Even today, the Lord's recovery is confronting opposition from traditional Christianity as the present evil age.

RELIGION BEING SOMETHING FOR GOD
YET APART FROM CHRIST
AND WITHOUT THE SPIRIT OF CHRIST

Religion is something for God and for the benefit of people, yet it is apart from Christ and without the Spirit of Christ. As long as Christ is not in something, no matter how good it may be, it is only religion. Even if we pray or study the Bible but are not in the spirit and do not have the Spirit of Christ, we are in religion, which does not bring forth the church. The Lord's recovery is to bring us back to the proper church life, and Christ as the Spirit is the only element that produces the church. As long as we do things in the spirit and with the Spirit of Christ, we have the church life. Otherwise, whatever we do may be good, may be for God, and may be for people's benefit, but we will simply produce another kind of religion. We all must pray, "Lord, be merciful to me that I would not do anything that produces a religion." Whatever we do must be realized and practiced in our spirit with the Spirit of Christ as the presence and reality of Christ.

We all need this revelation, and all the veils upon us need to be removed. Then we will see that what matters is not to have certain practices but to have the living Christ revealed in us (v. 16). Mere teaching is not able to help us. Rather, the more we speak, fellowship, and meet in the way of the church, the more the veils are removed and the more we receive a revelation in our spirit. God's desire is not a matter of religion but of the living Christ, the life-giving Spirit, dwelling in our human spirit. On his way to Damascus, Paul received not mere teaching but a revelation from the heavens so that he could see Christ and God's will to have the church, which comes out of Christ. At that time Paul became clear not by man's teaching but by a revelation of Christ from God. This is what we need today, and this is what the Lord is bringing to pass at this time.

Do not think that the Lord's recovery is here to produce another religion. If we are practicing even the best things in a religious way, we should give them up. Verse 15 of chapter 6 says, "Neither is circumcision anything nor uncircumcision, but a new creation is what matters." The new creation—the new man, the church—is produced only by Christ in our spirit. If we read Galatians again and pray-read the crucial verses in it, we will see that Christ is versus religion, and the church is versus traditions. Moreover, the proper gospel is not out of man but from God, and we receive it not by mere teaching but by revelation. In Galatians 1:15-16 Paul tells us that at a certain time it pleased God to reveal His Son in him. God's will today is to bring us back to Himself as the origin, the beginning, and to bring forth the church life by revealing Christ in us, not as an outward teaching but as an inward reality.

HAVING OUR ENTIRE BEING UNVEILED
TO SEE CHRIST AND RECEIVE HIM INTO US

God's will is simply to reveal His Son, Christ, in us. We need to leave behind the religious ways of meeting, praying, and teaching in today's Christianity. We should even leave behind our old traditional knowledge of the Bible. What we need is to have our entire being unveiled to see Christ and receive Him into us. As we experience the indwelling Christ's operating within us, we all love one another, and the result is that we have the church life. The church life is not a matter of religious teachings, gifts, regulations, forms, or ordinances. Galatians 3:28 says, "There cannot be Jew nor Greek, there cannot be slave nor free man, there cannot be male and female; for you are all one in Christ Jesus." Here there is nothing but Christ. Therefore, we should never argue about such matters as who is right and who is wrong. Both right and wrong avail nothing; Christ is everything.

We all, both young and old, must be saved from religion as the present evil age. May the Lord have mercy upon us so that our veils can be removed, that we may with unveiled face behold the living, indwelling, and transforming One to have a wonderful, direct fellowship with Him (2 Cor. 3:18). Out of this experience we will have the church life, not according to religious teachings, gifts, regulations, forms, or ordinances but by the indwelling Christ. It pleased God to reveal His Son in us, all our veils are being removed, and we see only God's eternal purpose—Christ and the church. We should not care for anything other than this.

CHAPTER TWO

LEAVING THE ORDINANCES OF RELIGION TO LIVE BY CHRIST AS OUR PERSON

Scripture Reading: Gal. 2:1-5, 11-14, 19-21

GOD'S INTENTION CONCERNING CHRIST AND THE CHURCH

God's intention is to impart Christ, the wonderful One, into His many believers so that He may have the church as a Body for Christ. His goal is to have a great universal man with Christ as the Head and the church as the Body (Eph. 2:15; Col. 2:19). He does not care for circumcision, the Sabbath, or ordinances concerning eating. He also does not care for methods of baptism, manners of head covering, whether or not we wash one another's feet, or whether we use grape juice or wine for the Lord's table. God cares only for Christ and the church. In the Old Testament, God commanded His people to practice circumcision, to keep the Sabbath, and to eat only clean things. On the eighth day after a Hebrew male was born, he had to be circumcised. Then every seven days a Jew needed to keep the Sabbath, and every day he had to follow the regulations concerning eating according to Leviticus 11. All these were required by the holy Word, and to keep these practices in the Old Testament age was absolutely right. Eventually, however, the Jews paid more attention to these matters than to God Himself, thus creating the outward religion of Judaism.

God had no intention to form a religion of circumcision, the Sabbath, and regulations concerning eating. His intention was to use circumcision as a type of dealing with the flesh, the Sabbath as a type of Christ being rest to people, and the regulations about eating as a type of our holy living in Christ in our contact with others (see Lev. 11 and footnotes in the Recovery Version). Not knowing this, however, the Jews received these outward items in the Word of God merely according to their human mentality and religious nature and formed them into a religion, while forgetting God Himself and neglecting His purpose.

JESUS COMING OUTSIDE OF THE JUDAISTIC RELIGION

In the fullness of times God came in the flesh, and He did not come in a religious way. The religious way of Judaism was a matter of the temple, the altar, the offerings, the priesthood, and regulations. The Jews supposed that these things were the way for them to contact God and the way for God to come to them. However, God came in an altogether different way. He came not in the temple but in a little manger, a crib where cattle are fed (Luke 2:7). Moreover, there were no priests present at His birth, nor were there the offerings of the altar. After His birth, this little babe did not go to Jerusalem. Instead, He went into Egypt, and after coming out from Egypt, He went to Galilee of the Gentiles, to the small town of Nazareth where He was raised (Matt. 2:13-15, 23). Nevertheless, this Jesus was none other than Jehovah God Himself. When Jesus was in Nazareth, God was there. If we were to seek God and worship Him at that time, we would have needed to go to Nazareth, not to Jerusalem. However, the religious people continued to go to Jerusalem because that is where the temple, the altar, the offerings, and the priests were. Moreover, when the Lord Jesus came out to work at the age of thirty, He did not go to the temple in Jerusalem but to the Jordan River to be baptized by John the Baptist, who lived outside of religion, wearing a garment of camel's hair and eating locusts and wild honey (3:1, 4, 13-17).

BEING SAVED FROM
THE PRESENT EVIL AGE OF RELIGION

The Jewish religion was built upon the three pillars of the Sabbath, regulations concerning eating, and circumcision. In the Gospels, when God came in the man Jesus, He tore down the first pillar by not observing the Sabbath in a religious way and even working on the Sabbath (12:1-2, 10-13; Luke 6:6-10). The Pharisees kept the Sabbath in a religious way, but Jesus abolished the outward observance of the Sabbath in a divine way. Then after the day of Pentecost, the Holy Spirit annulled the regulations concerning eating. When Peter went up on the housetop to pray, a trance came upon him in which a vessel like a great sheet descended, containing every manner of four-footed animals, reptiles, and birds (Acts 10:9-16). The animals symbolize men of all kinds, and the Lord's command to Peter to eat them indicated his need to contact every kind of unclean (sinful) man through the gospel; this began to be fulfilled at the house of Cornelius (vv. 15, 24, 27-28; Luke 13:29). The apostle Paul tore down the third pillar of Judaism by saying, "In Christ Jesus neither circumcision avails anything nor uncircumcision, but faith avails, operating through love" (Gal. 5:6; 6:15). In this way all three pillars of Judaism were torn down. Thus, Judaism in its entirety was finished, and now God is building up the church.

Not long after this, however, Christianity was formed as another religion with ordinances and regulations. In the ancient times the Jews paid their full attention to the things of Judaism and not to God and His purpose. Now, in the same principle, many people pay attention to Christianity as a religion rather than to Christ and the church. In these days the Lord desires to recover our experience of Christ and the proper practice of the church life. He is bringing us back to the beginning to have only Christ and the church. At the beginning of the church life, for example, the apostles baptized people, but there was no ordinance of baptism. Likewise, the New Testament does not give us ordinances and regulations related to the way to meet. However, religion has come in to frustrate people from God's purpose concerning Christ and the church. This religion is a strong veil that covers people, blinds them, and keeps them from a clear view of God's purpose. Even the knowledge and gifts mentioned in 1 Corinthians have been utilized by the enemy to veil the New Testament believers. For this reason, 2 Corinthians speaks of the veil of religion being taken away so that we may behold and reflect the glory of the Lord with an unveiled face (3:16-18). Then after 2 Corinthians comes the book of Galatians, which deals with religion and reminds us that God's intention is to have a pure and proper church life for Christ.

Galatians 1:4 says that Christ gave Himself for our sins that He might rescue us out of the present evil age. As we have seen, the present evil age refers to the religion of the present age, which today is Christianity. In Matthew 13:33 the Lord Jesus spoke of a woman who took leaven and hid it in three measures of meal until the whole was leavened. The unleavened fine flour signifies Christ as food to us, which is pure, holy, and divine. The woman signifies the Roman Catholic Church, which took in many pagan practices, heretical doctrines, and evil matters and mixed them with the teachings concerning Christ, leavening the whole content of Christianity (16:6, 11-12; 1 Cor. 5:6-8; Rev. 2:20). Not only the leaven but also the act of leavening are evil. This woman is seen again in Revelation as Jezebel (vv. 20-23) and ultimately as Babylon the Great, the mother of the harlots and abominations of the earth (17:1-5). Jezebel was surely evil, harlotry is evil, and from its beginning as Babel in Genesis 11 to its destruction in Revelation 17—19, Babylon is always considered as something evil. For this reason, we can definitely say that apostate Christianity is evil.

Although some may object to this teaching, we are simply burdened to speak the truth. We realize that within the Catholic Church and the denominations there are many real Christians, servants of the Lord. However, Revelation 17:4 tells us that Babylon is gilded with gold, precious stone, and pearls. Satan in his subtlety has utilized many saints to gild, to outwardly adorn, the evil woman. The New Jerusalem is not gilded but built up with these precious materials. The city proper of the New Jerusalem itself is gold from within to without (21:18-21). Babylon the Great, however, is merely gilded with gold as a pretense, presumption, hypocrisy, and falsehood, and the golden cup in her hand is full of abominations and the unclean things of her fornication (17:4). An abomination is an insult to God, and fornication damages the humanity made by God. This is truly evil.

Both the Catholic Church and the Protestant churches help people to know God and, to a certain extent, to be saved. However, God's purpose is not merely to gain a group of redeemed people. It is to gain the reality of the Body of Christ here on the earth today, expressed in the localities in which we live. In today's Christianity we cannot find the genuine work that cares for the present, practical building up of the church. Rather, many Christian teachers and leaders purposely do not touch the matter of the church. In a certain place to which I was invited to speak, my hosts told me, "Brother Lee, the believers in this city are very young and do not understand things clearly. We hope that you will simply minister life to them and not say anything about the church." For the first few days, I went along with this advice, but before the last meeting with them I was troubled. I realized that in order to be a faithful servant of the Lord, I should follow the Lord and speak concerning the church. Therefore, that evening I spoke concerning the Body of Christ in Romans 12. As a result, my hosts were grieved, and others too were offended. Nevertheless, one brother in the audience was captured; that brother is now a leading one among the churches in that area.

Christianity helps people to know God and even to be saved, but it does not help them to be saved to the fullest extent for the Body of Christ. After people receive this incomplete help from Christianity, it becomes a hindrance to them, frustrating them from going on in a fuller way to fulfill God's purpose. For this reason it is not the unbelievers or indifferent ones but certain religious Christians who criticize, condemn, and persecute the Lord's recovery today. This too demonstrates that the present age of religion is evil.

LEAVING THE ORDINANCES OF RELIGION
TO CARE ONLY FOR CHRIST AND THE CHURCH

Galatians 1 tells us that religion with its traditions persecutes the church, ravages it, and tries to uproot it (vv. 13-14). Following this, chapter 2 speaks clearly concerning the law with its ordinances. Paul begins this chapter by saying, "Then after a period of fourteen years I went up again to Jerusalem with Barnabas, taking Titus with me also. And I went up according to revelation" (vv. 1-2a). Paul went to Jerusalem not in a political way but according to and in obedience to a revelation from the Lord. Moreover, he took with him not only Barnabas, a Jew, but also Titus, an uncircumcised Gentile (v. 3). The Jewish believers in Jerusalem still esteemed the outward ordinance of circumcision. If Paul had gone to Jerusalem in the way of Judaistic teaching, he would not have gone with an uncircumcised Gentile for fear of offending the Jews. However, he went up in the way of revelation, taking Titus with him. For a Jew, it was not a small matter to give up the ordinances of the law. However, that no one compelled Titus to be circumcised means that Paul and those with him had given up the ordinances. Moreover, after Paul arrived, he did not seat Titus at a separate table when they ate (cf. vv. 11-13). This also proves that Paul acted not according to the politics and politeness of man but to a revelation from the Lord.

Christianity today is divided because of its many different ordinances. Some feel that it is normal to use musical instruments in the meetings, but others are offended by this, and as a result some Christian meetings have been divided. This demonstrates the problem with ordinances. In order for us to have the practical church life, all our ordinances need to go. Even some among us may still be holding on to their particular ordinances. Once a new one, who was a hippie, came into a meeting clothed with a large blanket. Because of the religious nature in certain ones and their ordinances concerning dress, they were bothered by this new one. In actuality, we cannot reject anyone simply because he dresses in a certain way. On another occasion, a number of saints who were burdened to leave their oldness behind had the feeling to be baptized a second time. Again, certain ones were bothered by this and began to criticize. We are not arguing for being baptized a second time. We are simply pointing out that these saints were touched by the Lord, and they were revived and living; moreover, many people came to the Lord through them. To oppose the Lord's spontaneous moving is to keep the old religious ordinances, which bring in spiritual death and dormancy.

Our living should be according to the holy Word, but we

should not make any point in the Word an ordinance to keep. Although we may practice a certain matter, to make it an ordinance that causes others to be excluded is wrong and annuls the church life. If the Lord delays His return, those who are young people today will one day bear the responsibility of the Lord's recovery. Therefore, they must all be clear that there should not be any ordinances in the church life. Some may feel to wash others' feet, but foot-washing must never become an ordinance. Likewise, the sisters may cover their head when they pray, but they must never make head covering an ordinance. It is the same with methods of baptism or whether or not to eat certain things. We all, including the young brothers and sisters among us, must be clear that in the Lord's recovery we do not hold on to ordinances. Rather, we care only for Christ and the church.

Peter had seen the vision on the Mount of Transfiguration, and he was a witness of the Lord's resurrection and ascension (Matt. 17:1-2; Mark 16:7; Acts 1:3, 9). Moreover, he had received the outpoured Spirit on the day of Pentecost and had seen the vision from the heavens concerning fellowship with the Gentiles (2:4, 14; 10:9-16). The visions that Peter saw were great, wonderful, and marvelous. In Galatians 2 Peter realized that he was free to eat with the uncircumcised Gentiles, and he practiced to do so. However, when some came from James, Peter began to shrink back and separate himself from the Gentiles. Moreover, the rest of the Jews, even Barnabas, joined him in this hypocrisy (vv. 12-13). At this point Paul opposed Peter to his face, rebuking him for not walking in a straightforward way in relation to the truth of the gospel (vv. 11, 14). It is almost incredible that Peter would practice hypocrisy in this way. This demonstrates how strong the influence of religion is.

LIVING NOT BY THE LAW BUT
BY THE INDWELLING CHRIST AS OUR PERSON

The Old Testament law was certainly good, but God's economy is not a matter of good or bad. God's economy is to dispense Christ into us so that we may be His corporate vessel, the Body of Christ, as His expression. To try to keep the law distracts people from God's economy. The law was simply a child conductor unto Christ to keep those whom God had predestinated for Christ and the church (3:24). We may compare the law to a mule cart. A mule cart is not bad, but today is the day of the jumbo jet. Because we have the "jumbo jet" of God's New Testament economy, we should no longer insist on keeping the "mule cart" of the law. The law was good, but today we have nothing to do with the old, outward law. Rather, we have been predestinated to receive Christ and become the members of His Body. Christ is the center of God's economy, and He is our destiny, our person, our life, and our everything. Do not argue whether the mule cart is right or wrong. We do not care for that. We are on the jumbo jet of God's economy.

Although we are no longer under the law given by Moses, we may still be under a self-made law. We may have made for ourselves many more than ten commandments concerning our personal life, our marriage life, and our work for the Lord, none of which we are able to keep. We need to leave all these behind so that we may care only for Christ. Galatians 2:19 says, "I through law have died to law that I might live to God." We are dead to the law, and now in resurrection we are living to God. We have nothing to do with the law; we have everything to do with God. Then in verse 20 Paul says, "I am crucified with Christ; and it is no longer I who live, but it is Christ who lives in me." This verse indicates that not only is Christ our life, but He also lives in us in a practical way.

The sisters should have no law as to where and when they should shop. Instead, they have Christ, who lives in them. To ask whether it is right or wrong to go shopping is to practice the law. Instead, we should check whether it is the Christ who lives in us or only we ourselves who want to go shopping. Many times the Lord's word to us is "No." If the Lord says no to our shopping, we also must say no. Then when is the right time to go shopping? It is when Jesus goes. Today we are living by Christ. If Christ wants to go to a certain place, we should go along with Him, but if He does not want to go, we can declare, "Hallelujah, it is no longer I, but it is Christ who lives in me." He is our life, and He is also our person as the One who lives in us. We are no longer in the realm of ordinances, law, regulations, or right and wrong. We are in another realm, the realm of Christ, who is the kingdom of God.

The proper church life issues from our experience of Christ living in us. From now, we should not ask whether it is right or wrong to wear a certain item or to do a certain thing. To ask in this way lacks the testimony of a person who lives Christ in the church life. Our living in the church is not a matter of law, ordinances, regulations, forms, or rituals. It is a matter only of Christ. Moreover, it is not a matter of what we do or do not do. It is altogether a matter of who does it— we or Christ. As long as Christ is doing something, we go along with Him. To live in this way is according to the revelation in Galatians. We have died to the law, and we are living to God. We are crucified with Christ, and it is no longer we who live, but it is Christ as our person who lives in us.

Chapter Three

CHRIST AS THE ALL-INCLUSIVE SPIRIT BEING THE BLESSING OF THE GOSPEL

Scripture Reading: Gal. 3:2-3, 5, 14

On the negative side, Galatians 1 exposes religion with its traditions, and chapter 2 speaks of the law with its ordinances. On the positive side, however, chapter 1 shows us Christ revealed in us, and chapter 2 unveils Christ living in us (1:15-16a; 2:20). We do not care for religion, even the religion of Christianity. We drop the "-anity" and keep only Christ, the One who is revealed in us and now lives in us. Moreover, Christ revealed in us and Christ living in us are for the church. Christ and the church are the contents of God's New Testament economy.

In chapter 3 the Spirit is mentioned four times: "Receive the Spirit...out of the hearing of faith" (v. 2); "having begun by the Spirit" (v. 3); "bountifully supplies to you the Spirit" (v. 5); and "receive the promise of the Spirit through faith" (v. 14). God promised the Spirit to us, we have received the ministered Spirit, and we have begun in the Spirit. Now we need to go on in the Spirit. This chapter also speaks of the flesh. Verse 3 says, "Having begun by the Spirit, are you now being perfected by the flesh?" Just as in chapter 1 Christ is in contrast with religion, in chapter 3 the Spirit is in contrast with the flesh. Both religion and the law are related to the flesh. After having begun in the Spirit, to make laws for ourselves is to try to perfect ourselves in the flesh. We need to forget about keeping the law in this way.

IN GALATIANS 3, CHRIST BEING THE ALL-INCLUSIVE SPIRIT

The way to leave the law behind and get out of the flesh is

to turn to the Spirit. Just as religion and the law are related to the flesh, Christ is related to the Spirit. In actuality, Christ is the Spirit (1 Cor. 15:45b; 2 Cor. 3:17). The very Christ in Galatians 1 and 2 is the Spirit in chapter 3. If Christ were not the Spirit, how could He be revealed in us and live in us? All Christians know that Christ died on the cross, was resurrected, and is now sitting on the throne in the third heaven, but if this were all, He would be far away from us and unable to live in us. However, Christ as the wonderful, all-inclusive Spirit today is like the air that we breathe (John 20:22). On the one hand, He is in the heavens, but on the other hand, He is also within us (Rom. 8:34, 10).

As the One who died on the cross for our sins, resurrected from the tomb, and ascended to heaven, He is Jesus Christ, but as the One who has come into us, He is also the Spirit. Christ is everything. He is the Father in eternity (Isa. 9:6), and in time He is the One who created the universe (Col. 1:16). He is also the One who came as a small child and was laid in a manger. He is the man Jesus who lived on earth, the redeeming Lamb of God that took away our sins on the cross, the Christ who resurrected to be our Savior, the Lord of all, who is sitting on the throne in the third heaven, and the coming King. He is the real God, the real man, life, light, wisdom, power, patience, kindness, love, and submission. Moreover, He is the Spirit who indwells us. From eternity to eternity Christ is everything and all-inclusive.

The revelation in Galatians is progressive. In chapters 1 and 2 the Lord is Christ, but in chapter 3 He is also the Spirit. We should never consider Christ and the Spirit to be separate. For redemption and as the One in the heavens, He is Christ, and for life imparting and as the One who indwells us, He is the Spirit.

BEING DELIVERED FROM THE FLESH
TO LIVE CHRIST IN THE SPIRIT

The positive factor in chapter 3 is the Spirit, and the negative factor is the flesh. The flesh here is simply the fallen man. Whether or not husbands love their wives and wives submit to their husbands, they still have the flesh. If some are proud, they have the flesh, and if others are humble, they also have the flesh. Likewise, whether or not someone keeps the law, he has the flesh. In this respect, there is no difference between people. If a tiger loves you or hates you, it is still a tiger. In the same principle, if a person loves or hates out from himself, he is still a person in the flesh. We need to be those who say, "Praise the Lord, I am not living in the flesh. By His mercy I am in the Spirit, and I live not by myself but by the Spirit."

In Luke 14:26 Jesus said, "If anyone comes to Me and does not hate his own father and mother and wife and children and brothers and sisters, and moreover, even his own soul-life, he cannot be My disciple." This indicates that we must not only love but also "hate" in a holy, divine way by the Spirit. What matters is not whether we love or hate but whether it is we or Christ as the Spirit who loves or hates. It must be no longer we who live but Christ who lives in us. God's salvation is not to save us from hell to heaven or from doing wrong to doing right. It is to save us from one person to another One, that is, from our self to Christ. However, we are too accustomed to being in our self. For this reason, God must come again and again in His mercy and grace to snatch us out of our self and bring us back into Christ.

We have been delivered out of the authority of darkness and transferred into the kingdom of the Son of His love (Col. 1:13), but practically speaking, we slip back into the old realm of our self many times, like someone who returns to his former home for a visit. Every husband has sinned against his wife, and every wife against her husband, simply because we are too often in the flesh. This is why we need to call, "O Lord Jesus." This is the simplest way to get out of the flesh and into the Spirit (1 Cor. 12:3b; Rom. 10:12-13).

TURNING FROM RELIGION IN OUR FLESH
TO THE CHRIST IN OUR SPIRIT
BY CALLING ON THE NAME OF THE LORD

There are always two realms before us—the realm of the flesh and the realm of the Spirit—which represent two possibilities for us. We may be in the realm of the Spirit one moment but immediately turn and be in the realm of the flesh the next moment. Therefore, we must call on the name of the Lord Jesus. It is not adequate even to pray, "O Lord, save me from my flesh. I would like to be in the Spirit, but I am about to lose my temper. O Lord, please help me." Even after praying like this, we may still lose our temper. The only way to quickly turn to the Spirit is to call, "O Lord Jesus. O Lord Jesus." To call on the Lord's name truly works. Whenever we call in this way, we are immediately in the realm of the Spirit.

Galatians 3 reveals both the Spirit and the flesh. Verse 3 says, "Are you so foolish? Having begun by the Spirit, are you now being perfected by the flesh?" We all need to answer, "O Lord, have mercy on me. I do not want to be so foolish as to seek perfection in the flesh." However, all Christians are foolish like this at some time. To make up our mind to do something or not to do it out of our own flesh is foolish. To say "I will never…" is not the realm we should be in. The realm we need to be in is the realm of the Spirit. We need to forget about ourselves, because we cannot do anything or be anything for the Lord unless we stay in the Spirit. We must not have any trust or confidence in ourselves. This does not mean that we are unable to love our wife, for example. A good gentleman can love his wife for a long time. Nevertheless, his love may simply be in the flesh. Whenever we try to do something for God by ourselves, we are religious and in the flesh. In this sense, to be religious is simply to be fleshly. Apparently, *religious* is a good word and *flesh* is not, but in practice both are equivalent.

If we are religious, we will try to adjust others. If someone is too quick and careless, we will exhort him to be slower and more cautious. However, if we have a proper vision, we will see that we do not need to be careless or more careful, quick or slow, and we do not need mere teaching. What we need is to receive the Spirit by calling on the Lord Jesus. Religion is related to the flesh and fits our natural tendency and the disposition of the flesh. Every husband, whether or not he is a Christian, realizes that he should love his wife, and every proper woman considers that she should submit to her husband. These inclinations are already in our nature. However, merely to follow our natural inclination is of the flesh and not out from the salvation in God's economy. God's economy is not that we give up evil things and do only good things. Even Confucius taught this to his disciples. God's economy is to dispense Christ, who is the life-giving Spirit, into us as our life and our person so that we would deny ourselves and follow the Christ who is within us, that is, in our human spirit (2 Tim. 4:22; Rom. 8:16). We should not look only to the Christ who is in heaven, and we should not try to find Him in the considerations and analysis of our mind. Rather, we should turn to our spirit and call, "O Lord Jesus."

THE SPIRIT BEING THE REALIZATION AND CONSUMMATION OF THE TRIUNE GOD

Galatians 3:8 says, "The Scripture, foreseeing that God would justify the Gentiles out of faith, announced the gospel beforehand to Abraham: 'In you shall all the nations be blessed.'" The gospel, which was first preached to Abraham, is that the nations are blessed in his seed, who is Christ (v. 16). To be blessed in Christ as the seed is not to go to heaven; heaven is not mentioned at all in this chapter. In Galatians 3 the blessing is the promised Spirit (v. 14). All the nations, the entire earth, are blessed in Christ with the promise of the Spirit. The Father is in the Son (John 14:10), and the Son is the all-inclusive Spirit (2 Cor. 3:17). Therefore, the Spirit is the Triune God Himself. The Triune God is the Father, the Son, and the Spirit, but this does not mean that we have three Gods; there is only one God (Gal. 3:20; Deut. 6:4; Rom. 3:30; 1 Cor. 8:6; James 2:19). We must be careful even in using terms such as the "persons" in the Godhead. W. H. Griffith Thomas, the writer of a top exposition on Romans, wrote that our human language is inadequate to explain the mystery of the Divine Trinity. In his book *The Principles of Theology,* he writes, "The term 'Person' is also sometimes objected to...It certainly must not be pressed too far, or it will lead to Tritheism." Nevertheless, the teaching of the Divine Trinity that the three in the Godhead are separate gives the impression of tritheism—that the Father, the Son, and the Spirit are three separate Gods.

We believe in the Triune God—the Father, the Son, and the Spirit (Matt. 28:19). However, we cannot systematize Him, and our human words are inadequate to describe Him. In Isaiah 9:6 the Son who is given to us is called Eternal Father. In John 14:8 Philip said, "Lord, show us the Father and it is sufficient for us." Jesus said to him, "Have I been so long a time with you, and you have not known Me, Philip? He who has seen Me has seen the Father; how is it that you say, Show us the Father? Do you not believe that I am in the Father and the Father is in Me?" (vv. 9-10a). To see Brother Jones is to see Mr. Jones. It is foolish to say to Brother Jones, "Show us Mr. Jones." Likewise, to see Jesus is to see the Father, because He is in the Father and the Father is in Him. Moreover, 1 Corinthians 15:45b says, "The last Adam [Christ the Son] became a life-giving Spirit," and 2 Corinthians 3:17 says, "The Lord is the Spirit." We believe Matthew 28:19, which speaks of the Father, the Son, and the Holy Spirit, and we also believe Isaiah 9:6, John 14:9-10a, 1 Corinthians 15:45b, and 2 Corinthians 3:17.

The Spirit today is the realization and consummation of the entire Triune God, and the Triune God bountifully supplies Himself to us as the Spirit (Gal. 3:5). This Spirit is all-inclusive; the fullness of the Godhead, divinity, humanity, crucifixion, resurrection, ascension, and all positive things are included in this Spirit. When we receive this Spirit, we receive everything we need. We receive the Creator, divinity, humanity, the Redeemer, the Lamb of God, the resurrected Christ, the ascended Christ, salvation, life, light, love, and all positive things. All these items are in the Spirit, who has been ministered and is still being ministered to us.

THE BLESSING OF THE GOSPEL
BEING THE ALL-INCLUSIVE SPIRIT

The Spirit is ministered to us through the death of Christ on the cross. Christ died on the cross in order that we may receive the blessing of Abraham, the bountiful Spirit (vv. 13-14). The greatest blessing is not to receive a high degree, or to have a good husband or wife, good job, good car, and good house. It is not even to have our sins forgiven and to go to heaven.

The greatest blessing is to receive the Triune God as the all-inclusive Spirit. This inclusive Spirit includes the eternal Father, the Creator, the incarnated God, the man Jesus, the Lamb of God, the Redeemer, the resurrected Christ, the Savior, Master, King of kings, and Lord of lords. What a blessing this is! The blessing of the gospel is not merely forgiveness of sins and regeneration, followed by peace, happiness, comfort, and the hope of heaven. The blessing of the gospel is the all-inclusive Spirit.

On the negative side, Galatians 1:4 tells us that Christ gave Himself for our sins that He might rescue us out of the present evil age. Then on the positive side, 3:13 and 14 say that Christ redeemed us in order that we may receive the promised Spirit as the blessing of Abraham. Now religion is over, and the Spirit has come. We are through with religion, and we are now in the Spirit. All the Jews must forget Judaism, and the Christians should no longer care for traditional Christianity. Nothing is worth holding on to. We care only for the Spirit. Having begun by the Spirit, we should not foolishly seek to be perfected by the flesh. We should simply remain in the all-inclusive Spirit who dwells in us. If we do this, the Bible will become fresh, living, strengthening, and stirring to us; it will never be a book of dead letters. Moreover, it will become food to nourish and satisfy us, and day by day we will grow in the divine life and be transformed. Then it will be no longer we who live but Christ who lives in us.

THE ISSUE OF OUR EXPERIENCE OF CHRIST AS THE SPIRIT BEING THE BUILDING UP OF THE CHURCH AS THE BODY OF CHRIST

The issue and outcome of our experience of Christ as the Spirit is the building up of the church as the Body of Christ. The Lord is recovering Christ as our life and our person in our experience so that we may have the proper, practical, present, and constant church life. The Lord does not intend to recover mere doctrinal teachings, particular practices, or forms. He is recovering our experience of the real, living, indwelling Christ as the all-inclusive Spirit so that we may have a practical daily life in the Spirit and spontaneously become the one

Body expressed as the local churches in every locality that we are in. This kind of real, living, and practical church life will push the enemy into the "corner." It will give the Lord the standing to boast, "Satan, look at the churches. You have been trying for twenty centuries to damage the building up of My church, but now My church is being built up. Look at these 'crazy' lovers of Me. They do not care for practices, gifts, or mere doctrinal teachings. They do not care even for spirituality or for going to heaven. Instead, they are simply being built up together as My church. You can never prevail against this. If you touch the church, you will be defeated." The Lord will build up His church, and this built-up church will be the stepping stone for His coming back. When the building up of the local churches is complete, the Lord will say, "Satan, now is My time to return." At that time Satan will have nothing to say. He will be defeated. He will be put to shame, and the Lord Jesus will have the glory.

Today in Christianity people hold on to ordinances, particular doctrines, and certain gifts, which have resulted in division and confusion. However, the Lord is rescuing many out of division and confusion to stand simply for Christ and the church. After a number of years the whole earth will be filled with built-up churches. Throughout America, Europe, and many places, the churches will be built up in a glorious and wonderful way. We will no longer care for religion with its traditions, the law with its ordinances, the self, or the flesh. We will simply have Christ as the Spirit for the church life. The Lord will accomplish this in His recovery.

CHAPTER FOUR

ENJOYING THE ALL-INCLUSIVE CHRIST TO INHERIT THE PROMISE OF THE SPIRIT

Scripture Reading: Gal. 3:23-29; 4:4-10, 19, 21-31

GOD'S PURPOSE BEING
TO WORK THE ALL-INCLUSIVE CHRIST INTO US

God's purpose is to work Christ into us. The entire Bible reveals that this Christ is all-inclusive. As God, Christ is the eternal Father. Isaiah 9:6 says, "A child is born to us, / A Son is given to us; / And the government / Is upon His shoulder; / And His name will be called / Wonderful Counselor, / Mighty God, / Eternal Father, / Prince of Peace." The Son given to us is called Eternal Father. As God, Christ is also the Creator (Col. 1:16; John 1:3). In time He was incarnated to be a man (v. 14), who was crucified on the cross as the Lamb of God to be our Redeemer (v. 29). Following this, He rose from the dead, and as the resurrected One He is our living Savior (Acts 5:31; 13:23). He died on the cross to redeem us from our sins, and now He lives as the Savior to deliver us from every sinful thing. Moreover, in resurrection, through resurrection, and by resurrection this wonderful Jesus became the life-giving Spirit (1 Cor. 15:45b; 2 Cor. 3:17). Now as the ascended One, the One who was raised to the third heaven and seated on the throne of God, He is the Lord and Christ (Acts 2:36), the One appointed and anointed by God to execute all that God planned to do for the accomplishment of His purpose. (The Greek name *Christos* means "the anointed One.")

God was incarnated to be a man by the name of Jesus, which means "Jehovah the Savior" (Matt. 1:21). Since Jesus is not only Jehovah but also Jehovah becoming our salvation, we may say that He is "Jehovah plus." Furthermore, Jesus is also called Emmanuel, which means "God with us" (v. 23). Again we may say that Jesus is "God plus." The Jews have Jehovah, and they have God, but we have Jehovah plus and God plus, that is, Jehovah the Savior and God with us. All the foregoing items are related to Christ as a person. In addition, Christ is light, life, power, wisdom, righteousness, sanctification, redemption, our spiritual food, our spiritual drink, and our spiritual breath, as well as our practical virtues, such as kindness, humility, and patience (John 8:12; 1:4; 1 Cor. 1:24, 30; 10:3-4; John 20:22). Jesus Christ is all-inclusive.

THE ALL-INCLUSIVE CHRIST
BEING THE TOTALITY OF THE TRIUNE GOD

Some who are shortsighted claim that Christ is only the Son, not the Father or the Spirit. If Christ were not the Father and the Spirit, He would not be all-inclusive. Only by being the Son, the Father, the Spirit, man, the Lamb of God, the Redeemer, the Savior, the Lord, the Master, and so many items can He be all in all. The holy Word tells us that Jesus is even signified by the earth. Like plants, we are living organisms as God's farm (1 Cor. 3:9); as such, we have been rooted in Christ (Col. 2:7), our soil, our earth, so that we may absorb all His riches as our nourishment. Similarly, Christ is also signified by heaven. In Luke 15:21 the prodigal son confessed to his father, "Father, I have sinned against heaven and before you." To sin against heaven is to sin against God. Heaven represents God, and God is Christ. Our real heaven is Christ. If our real heaven were not Christ, we would not care to go there. We may compare this to a small babe, who does not care where he is; he cares only that his mother is there. Likewise, we do not care to go anywhere, even to heaven, apart from Jesus. Rather, wherever Jesus is, that is heaven to us. When Jesus was laid in a manger, even that small place became heaven. If Jesus had not been there, that manger would have meant nothing to the magi from the east or to the shepherds (Matt. 2:9-11; Luke 2:8-12).

We should not listen to the traditional teaching that the

three persons of the Godhead revealed in Matthew 28:19 are three separate Gods. According to the wrong concept conveyed by the traditional teaching in Christianity, many believe that the Father is one God, the Son is another God, and the Spirit is yet another God. We receive the pure Word, which says, "Baptizing them into the name of the Father and of the Son and of the Holy Spirit" (v. 19), and thus we believe that God is triune, but we do not believe that there are three Gods. Rather, the Father, the Son, and the Spirit are three in one and one in three. John 1:1 says, "In the beginning was the Word, and the Word was with God, and the Word was God." Are God and the Word one or two? This is wonderful but too difficult for our natural mentality to fully comprehend.

When possible, we prefer not even to use the word *persons* when referring to the three of the Godhead, because the Bible does not use this word when speaking of God. God is a mystery. Even we ourselves are a mystery, and we cannot understand ourselves adequately. Jeremiah 17:9 says, "The heart is deceitful above all things, / And it is incurable; / Who can know it?" According to the Bible and according to our experiences, we have two hearts; one is the physical heart, and the other is our psychological heart. We know where our physical heart is, but no one can say where our psychological heart is. Moreover, we have a soul and a spirit, and we have a mind and a will, yet we do not know where they are within us. All this proves that we do not understand ourselves. Therefore, we should not try to understand the mysterious God. Nevertheless, we know that God is real. We cannot fully understand Him, but we can receive Him according to His pure Word.

CHRIST BEING THE FATHER, THE SON, AND THE SPIRIT

In the King James Version, Romans 8:16 renders the pronoun for the Spirit as "itself," leaving the impression that the translators of that version did not realize that the Holy Spirit is a person, considering Him simply as a kind of power or instrument. From the time of the American Standard Version of 1901, people began to see more clearly that the Holy Spirit is a divine person, so that at least since then, translations refer to the Spirit as "He" or "Himself." However, some of the

Brethren continued to teach that we should not pray to the Holy Spirit but only to the Father and sometimes to the Lord. I myself was taught in this way, because I was under the teaching of the Brethren for seven years. I adopted their teaching, and I tried to practice it. Many times I began my prayer by saying, "O Father in heaven." Then after a few minutes I realized that the One to whom I was praying is not only in heaven but also within me. At this point I might pray, "O Lord, O Father, my Lord." I was very bothered when this happened, wondering whether He is the Father or the Lord. After this, I was more cautious when I prayed, carefully considering whether I should pray to the Father or to the Lord. This demonstrates that we have been too influenced by the traditional teaching of Christianity.

In 1933 I gave up my job and went to Shanghai, China, to visit Brother Watchman Nee. He received me as his guest and also as his trainee for four months. One day Brother Nee invited a traveling preacher from the China Inland Mission churches to give a message in our meeting. At a certain point in his message, the preacher said, "Please, do not think that Jesus is one and the Holy Spirit is another. You must all realize that the Lord Jesus and the Spirit are one. Today Jesus the Lord is the Holy Spirit." Brother Nee, who was sitting in the back of the meeting, boldly said Amen! That surprised us all very much. After that meeting, while dinner was being prepared, Brother Nee took me on a little walk. I took the opportunity to ask him why he had so boldly said Amen. He told me, "This message is what we need. It is right to say that the Lord Jesus is the Holy Spirit."

Because there were not many saints in the Lord's recovery at that time, the work among us was not great. This gave Brother Nee the time to sit with the eight or ten trainees living there and have some free talk. This went on for a long period of time. These were wonderful times, and I can never forget them. At a certain point he was burdened to expound John 14 to us. Formerly, the Brethren had taught me mostly concerning types and prophecies, such as the seventy weeks and the ten toes, four beasts, seven heads, and ten horns (Dan. 9:24; 2:34; 7:2-3; Rev. 13:1; 17:3). At this time, however,

Brother Nee sat down to speak something more profound from John 14. He pointed out how Philip foolishly asked Jesus, "Lord, show us the Father and it is sufficient for us" (v. 8). Jesus answered, "Have I been so long a time with you, and you have not known Me, Philip? He who has seen Me has seen the Father; how is it that you say, Show us the Father? Do you not believe that I am in the Father and the Father is in Me?" (vv. 9-10a). The Lord seemed to be saying, "Don't you know by now that if you see Me, you see the Father? You have seen the Father every day for several years. The Father is in Me, and I am in the Father. We are one." Verse 16 continues, "I will ask the Father, and He will give you another Comforter, that He may be with you forever." Then in verse 18 the pronoun changes from *He* to *I:* "I will not leave you as orphans; I am coming to you." *He* (the Comforter) in verse 16 is *I* (Jesus) in verse 18. Therefore, the Lord Jesus is not only the Father but also the Spirit. We must receive this word, because it is the word of the Bible in John 14. When Brother Nee shared this with us, my eyes became open. This was truly new to me.

We do not teach in a light way that Christ is the Son, the Father, and also the Spirit. We have spent many years studying this matter in the Bible and in our experience. The New Testament tells us that the Father is in us (Eph. 4:6), the Son is in us (2 Cor. 13:5; Col. 1:27), and the Spirit is in us (John 14:17). According to our experience, do we have three or one in us? In John 14:23 Jesus said, "If anyone loves Me, he will keep My word, and My Father will love him, and We will come to him and make an abode with him." Here the Lord said that "We," the Father and the Son, will abide in the disciples. However, it is not accurate to say that two or three dwell in us, because the Father, the Son, and the Spirit are one.

Shortly before Brother Nee was imprisoned, he wrote a hymn that says,

> Thou, Lord, the Father once wast called,
> But now the Holy Spirit art;
> The Spirit is Thine other form,
> Thyself to dwell within our heart.
>
> (*Hymns,* #490)

Later, after we came to Taiwan, we further saw the truth in 1 Corinthians 15:45b, which says, "The last Adam became a life-giving Spirit." At that time the light shined brightly from this verse. About the same time we also saw 2 Corinthians 3:17: "The Lord is the Spirit." We looked into many different translations to find the correct rendering of this verse. We found that John N. Darby, in his New Translation, places verses 7 through 16 in parenthesis, meaning that in Darby's realization, verse 17 directly continues verse 6. Verse 6 says, "The letter kills, but the Spirit gives life," and verse 17 continues, "The Lord is the Spirit." The Lord in verse 17 is the Spirit who gives life in verse 6.

DRINKING OF THE ALL-INCLUSIVE CHRIST AS THE ALL-INCLUSIVE SPIRIT WHO DWELLS IN US

The traditional theology of today's fundamental Christianity is not altogether accurate. Therefore, we should not remain in it but should return to the pure Word of God to see that our Jesus, whom God is working into us, is all-inclusive. This means that all that Christ is in many items and aspects is being wrought into us. This is God's purpose. God does not intend that we keep the Sabbath, the law, the ordinances, or many other items of practice. Neither is it that we hold to a religion with its teachings and traditions. God's intention is to work Christ as the all-inclusive Spirit into us. We may compare Christ as the Spirit to an all-inclusive drink with many healthy ingredients combined together. We have all been given to drink one Spirit (1 Cor. 12:13). In this all-inclusive Spirit whom we drink is God, the Father, the Creator, the man Jesus, the Lamb of God, the Redeemer, the Savior, life, love, light, wisdom, power, sanctification, holiness, and patience. When we drink of Him by calling, "O Lord Jesus," we take in every positive item (v. 3b).

Holiness is not a kind of sinless perfection, as John Wesley taught. Rather, holiness is Christ, who is our life (Col. 3:4). Life, holiness, comfort, and consolation are all Christ, who is the all-inclusive Spirit today. When we are troubled, tested, and suffering, we need consolation. At these times we need to call, "O Lord Jesus." Then we will experience true consolation and refreshment. Jesus is so many items to us. When a mother is troubled by her children, or a wife by her husband, she simply needs to take Jesus as her all-inclusive drink. No one but Jesus can truly solve our problems, answer our questions, or be our true consolation. We all need to take a drink of the all-inclusive Christ by calling, "O Lord Jesus, O Lord Jesus." I am frequently asked by the churches to give a conference, and very often I am not clear as to what I should minister. At these times I do not merely consult with certain books. Rather, I take a few "cups" of Jesus as the all-inclusive drink by calling on Him. Then I become clear, and I receive something to minister to people. God's purpose is to work the all-inclusive Christ as the all-inclusive Spirit into us.

BECOMING THE CHURCH BY BEING ONE IN CHRIST

The proper church life comes not out of religion, ordinances, and the law but from the very Christ whom we experience. In the book of Galatians, *church* and *churches* are mentioned only in chapter 1 (vv. 2, 13, 22). Practically speaking, however, this book uses a number of synonyms for the church. Verse 28 of chapter 3 says, "You are all one in Christ Jesus." This oneness is the church. As the church, we are all one by being baptized into Christ and putting on Christ (v. 27). However, today's Christianity is fully divided by ordinances, doctrinal teachings, and gifts. In ordinances we are different and divided. Some hold to the practice of foot-washing, head covering, and certain forms of baptism, whereas others do not. Similarly, some hold to particular teachings concerning many matters, and others do not hold the same teachings; moreover, some practice certain gifts, but others do not. Differing ordinances, opinions, teachings, and gifts are all causes of division. In His recovery the Lord will deliver many people from their divisions in differing ordinances, doctrines, traditions, practices, and gifts to practice the oneness in Christ. We all need to remain in Christ and care only for Christ and the church.

THE LAW BEING A GUARDIAN AND A CHILD-CONDUCTOR TO BRING US TO CHRIST

Verse 14 says that we have received the promise of the

Spirit through faith. This Spirit is Christ, into whom we have been baptized and whom we have put on (v. 27). We can be baptized into Christ because, as the Spirit, He is the living water into whom we are immersed. Now we all are in Christ. The Judaizers might have asked, "What then is the purpose of the law, and why did God give it to us?" The law was given as a guardian before Christ came in order to keep His chosen people, just as a sheepfold keeps the flock safe at night, during storms, and in the winter (John 10:1, 9). Eventually, when Christ came, the law functioned as a child-conductor to bring people to Him (Gal. 3:23-24). In the ancient days a guardian cared for a child who was under age and conducted him to the schoolmaster. The law kept God's people before Christ came and conducted them to Him after His coming. At this point the law was finished and had no further position. Accordingly, there is no further need for religion. Therefore, we should no longer hold to the law, ordinances, and traditions. Today we have only Christ as our living Teacher. We are in Him, and He is in us.

EXPERIENCING CHRIST AS GRACE
AND BEING DEAD TO THE LAW

When the law was rightly used, it served as a guardian and a child-conductor, as revealed in Galatians 3. In the negative sense, however, the law was a concubine, illustrated by Hagar in chapter 4. Both the position and the function of a concubine are wrong. The law should be only a guardian and a child-conductor; it should never bring forth children. Once the law produces children, it becomes a concubine, and what she produces are not children of promise but children unto slavery (vv. 24, 28). Verse 30 says, "Cast out the maidservant and her son." This is to cast out the law with all that the law produces. Paul tells us that the allegory of the two women portrays two covenants, the covenant of grace and the covenant of law. The first covenant, that of grace and portrayed by Sarah, was given to Abraham, to whom God preached the gospel (3:8). Then after more than four hundred years, the second covenant, that of the law and portrayed by Hagar, was given at Mount Sinai. God did not acknowledge Ishmael, the son produced by Hagar, and He did not recognize him as a proper heir. Rather, He told Abraham to cast out the maidservant and her son. God acknowledged only Isaac, the one who was begotten of Sarah according to the promise, as the one who would inherit the promised blessing of the Spirit.

We may illustrate the principle of the two covenants as follows. Ephesians 5:22 says, "Wives, be subject to your own husbands as to the Lord," and verse 25 continues, "Husbands, love your wives even as Christ also loved the church and gave Himself up for her." After reading this, a husband may make up his mind to endeavor to love his wife, and to some extent he may be able to do it. Similarly, after reading verse 22 a sister may endeavor to submit to her husband. She may tell her husband, "Whatever you say, I will do it, and if you don't agree, I will not do it." For a certain period of time she too may be successful. However, the husband's love and his wife's submission are "Ishmael," not "Isaac," because they are produced according to the principle of law. Such love and submission may be real, just as Ishmael was a real child, but God will say, "Cast them out." If our eyes are opened to see this, we will realize that God rejects not only hatred and rebellion but also the love and submission that come out of the self trying to keep the law.

We should not think that there are only ten commandments in the Bible. Many Christians have converted almost the entire New Testament into commandments. Where then is the real experience of Isaac? A certain brother may not know how to interpret Ephesians 5:25, but he realizes that Jesus is in him, and he knows how to drink the living Spirit by calling, "O Lord Jesus." In this way, Christ as love spontaneously flows out of him to his wife. This is the genuine experience of Isaac, symbolizing the children of promise born out of grace. The law was not intended to be kept. If we try to keep the law, we misuse it and make it a concubine to produce an Ishmael. The law was simply meant to be a guardian and a child-conductor to keep us and to bring us to Christ. Once this is accomplished, we can say good-bye to the law, because it has no further position and function. We are dead to the law, and we are living to God (Gal. 2:19).

CHAPTER FIVE

PRACTICING THE GENUINE CHURCH LIFE BY LIVING AND WALKING BY THE SPIRIT

Scripture Reading: Gal. 5:1-2, 4-6, 11, 13, 16-25

Galatians is a book on Christ versus many negative matters, such as the law with all the ordinances, religion with traditions, and the flesh. As long as we hold to one of these negative things, we are through with Christ in a practical way. If we try to keep the law with its ordinances, we are deprived of all profit from Christ (5:2), and if we still hold on to the traditions of religion, we are brought to nought and separated from Christ (v. 4). Moreover, if we live by the flesh, we are not living by Christ as the life-giving Spirit indwelling our spirit (vv. 16-17). On the negative side, Galatians exposes religion, traditions, the law, ordinances, and the flesh, and on the positive side, it shows us Christ for the producing of the church.

Each of the first four chapters of Galatians reveals a particular aspect of Christ. In chapter 1, Christ is revealed in us (vv. 15a, 16a). In chapter 2, Christ lives in us (v. 20). In chapter 3, we have been baptized into Christ and have put Him on (v. 27). At this point, Christ is in us, and we are in Christ. Then in chapter 4, this Christ needs to be formed within us. Verse 19 says, "My children, with whom I travail again in birth until Christ is formed in you." This is a strong word. Christ not only is revealed in us, is living in us, and is put upon us, but He is also being formed in us. This means that He is mingled with us. Our entire being with all its inward parts—our spirit, mind, will, and emotion—becomes the dwelling place of Christ.

We may illustrate our need for Christ to be formed in us with a hand and a glove. If only the tips of the fingers are in the glove, we still can say that the "hand" is in the glove, but this is not adequate. In the same way, we may declare that Christ lives in us, but He may not thoroughly dwell in us. For this reason, Paul travailed in birth that Christ would be formed in the believers. To travail is to labor much with suffering and struggling. After much travailing, Christ will be formed in us in a thorough way. Then we will be truly one with Him, and He will be one with us. Christ will make His home in every aspect, area, and avenue of our inward parts. This is altogether a matter of Christ being revealed in us, living in us, being put upon us, and being formed in us.

The experience of Christ in Galatians is not a matter of doing good or of keeping the law with its ordinances, religion with its traditions, or any rituals, forms, and regulations. Rather, Galatians shows us that we need to drop all these things. We need to leave the law behind, drop the ordinances, cast out religion, bury the traditions, and crucify the flesh. The Christian life is a matter only of Christ, not in an objective way but in a very subjective way. He is our life, our person, and the content of all our inward parts. Christ must be fully formed in every area of our being. Then we will be not only sons of God but also heirs of God, inheriting all that God is for our enjoyment (4:7). We do not care for the law, because we have God in Christ. We do not have a religion; we have Christ with all that God is. Moreover, we do not hold to traditions and ordinances; instead, we have the unsearchable riches of Christ (Eph. 3:8).

THE PRACTICALITY OF THE CHURCH LIFE
BEING CHRIST AS OUR ONENESS

Because we drop all the negative matters and hold only to Christ, we are not confused and divided. Rather, we all are one in Christ. This oneness is the practicality of the church life. Formerly, many of us were scattered in the denominations and free groups. However, we can now boast to Satan, saying, "Look at the oneness in the churches today. All the different kinds of people are one in Christ." We are one not in doctrines, the law, ordinances, religion, traditions, or any fleshly similarity. We are one in Christ. If all the real Christians would be like this, the kingdom of the heavens would spread throughout the earth. In this case, there would be no need for the United Nations. The earth does not need that kind of oneness. The true oneness is in the church life. The Lord will recover and carry out this oneness, not with the majority of Christians but with a minority as a remnant, in the principle of the overcomers.

We may compare the recovery of the church life to the reformation of the nation of Israel. Israel was reformed not with all the Jews on the earth but with only a minority. There are millions of Jews in New York City alone, but they are not the nation of Israel. The nation of Israel is composed of only the relatively few who returned to the land of their forefathers, remained there, and built it up. In the same principle, there are millions of Christians today, but as long as they are scattered, divided, and confused, they are not the church in practicality. Just as the Jews in New York City are true Jews, all genuine Christians are the members of the Body of Christ, but most of them are still scattered. However, a minority, a small number, a remnant, has been rescued from the divisions and confusion as well as from laws, ordinances, religion, and traditions. The Lord Jesus has gathered us here together as one. As long as we stand in this oneness, we can tell others, "Come and see. This is the church!"

Some may ask, "Since we are real Christians, are we not also the church?" To be sure, all the saved ones are genuine Christians, but many are still scattered in the denominations and divisions. If they would be rescued from the divisions, they will return to the practicality of the Body, where Christ Himself is our oneness. We ourselves may still be accustomed to certain kinds of ordinances, particularly in the practice of our meetings. However, we must avoid every ordinance, even those that appear to be good. We are here only for Christ as our oneness. This is the way of the Lord's recovery today. The Lord is recovering the proper church life, which is a life with Christ, by Christ, in Christ, and for Christ.

WALKING BY THE SPIRIT AND
BEING ONE SPIRIT WITH THE LORD

After Galatians 1 through 4, the emphasis of chapter 5 is no longer on the law, ordinances, religion, and traditions. Rather, this chapter speaks of walking by the Spirit, living by the Spirit, and being led by the Spirit (vv. 16, 25, 18). It is difficult for translators of the Bible to decide whether *Spirit* refers to the Holy Spirit or to our human spirit. According to the context, the Spirit here is the Holy Spirit, who dwells in and mingles with our regenerated spirit. Again, we may use a hand in a glove as an illustration. The gloved hand is neither a hand alone nor simply a glove, because the two have become one. Christ as the divine Spirit, the life-giving Spirit, is mingled with our spirit. As we have seen, Christ is revealed in us, He lives in us, we have put Him on, and He is now being formed in us. As a result, we two are one; He becomes us, and we become Him. The Lord is the Spirit, and the Spirit is mingled with our spirit to be one spirit (2 Cor. 3:17; Rom. 8:16). This oneness is not a matter of our natural mind, heart, or flesh but of the Spirit in our spirit, as 1 Corinthians 6:17 says, "He who is joined to the Lord is one spirit." He and we, we and He, are now one spirit.

Now, whatever we do, we must do it in the mingled spirit. We leave behind all the negative things—the law, ordinances, religion, traditions, and the flesh—and we remain in the mingled spirit. This is why after Galatians deals with so many negative matters, the last portion of chapter 5 emphasizes only the Spirit. Day by day we need to walk by the Spirit in our spirit, be led by the Spirit, and have our life in the Spirit. We do not need to ask whether we should do one thing or the other. We must simply walk by the Spirit and be led by Him. If the Spirit leads one way, we do that, but if He leads another way, we do that instead. Many years ago when brothers and sisters would come to ask me for advice, I would have much to say to them. However, today I am much simpler. If someone asks me to fellowship with them for half an hour, I am often clear that the answer to their question will take closer to half a minute. The answer to many questions is simply, "Go according to the Spirit in your spirit." If we would do everything according to the Spirit in our spirit, we will be freed from problems and saved from turmoil.

Many dear ones ask me, "Brother Lee, your burden is so heavy. Are you afflicted and have many worries?" On the contrary, I remain joyful and healthy. Worry comes not from the spirit but from the mind. Similarly, anger comes from our emotions. If we remain in our mind, worries come to us, and if we stay in our emotions, we become bothered and lose our temper. However, if we walk by the Spirit, all our worries and anger are gone.

The traditional teachings of Christianity have made the experience of Christ to appear too complicated. Instead, it is very simple. We may compare the Spirit in our spirit to electricity. Once electricity is installed in a building, the building has whatever we need. If we need heat, we can plug in a heater, and if we need light, we can simply flip a switch. Christ as the Spirit today is the "electricity" within us, providing us with everything that we need, and our spirit is the "switch" to turn Him on within us. We must be unloaded of all our negative burdens. In the Lord's recovery we must not care for the law, ordinances, religion, traditions, or the flesh. We care only for Christ as the life-giving Spirit who indwells our spirit, causing these two spirits to be one. We can turn on the "switch" of our spirit by calling on His name to enjoy Him as the divine electricity.

COMING TO THE BIBLE AND CONTACTING THE LORD BY PRAYING IN THE MINGLED SPIRIT

When I was young, I would buy many books, especially expositions of the Bible. Whenever I studied a certain part of the Bible, I would spread out my books on my desk, my bed, and even on the floor. I also used different Greek lexicons and concordances of the Bible. I liked to compare, investigate, study, search, and research in this way. Today, however, I prefer to open the Word, choose a few verses, and enjoy them by praying in the mingled spirit. When we pick up Galatians, we may pray, "There are no more ordinances. Amen. No more law. Amen. No more religion. Amen. There is only Christ revealed in me, living in me, put upon me, and formed in me.

Amen. Today this Christ is the Spirit in my spirit. Oh, these two spirits are mingled as one. Hallelujah!" By praying in this way we will receive much nourishment.

Some Christians today do not pray enough, but others pray with too many stories for the Lord and many details concerning persons, places, activities, and intentions. Our Father in heaven already knows the things that we need. Therefore, we should forsake the way of telling the Lord stories. To pray in this way is tiring, and it wastes the Lord's time and ours. If someone prays like this, he may even become bored with his prayer. On the one hand, he will feel that he needs to pray, but on the other hand, his prayer will be burdensome. Eventually, he may go for a long time with no prayer at all. Then he will say, "Father, I repent. I did not pray for three weeks. Forgive me. From today on, I will recover my prayer life." After this, he will begin to pray again, but he will do it in the same, old way. This is the practice of the law, ordinances, religion, traditions, and the flesh. Even when we come to the dining table, we may give a word of grace in a traditional way, praying in the same way time after time. This also is a practice of religion. We need to drop the old way of prayer. When we come to eat, we may simply feel to say, "Amen! Praise the Lord!"

PRACTICING THE GENUINE CHURCH LIFE
BY LIVING AND WALKING BY THE SPIRIT

God's way is marvelous. It is simple, living, powerful, refreshing, strengthening, and life-giving. We have no need for a religion. Nevertheless, our human nature cares not for the Spirit in our spirit but for culture, the law, ordinances, religion, and traditions. From the day we were born, our spirit was dormant within us, but one day the Lord Jesus woke up our spirit by entering into it. However, the more Christians exercise their mind over lifeless doctrines, the more their spirit "goes to sleep" again. Then as they pick up more religious teachings and practices, they become more divided. This is not the Lord's way. By the last portion of Galatians 5, the emphasis is no longer on the negative things of religion. All that we have is the Spirit mingled with our spirit. "If we live by the Spirit, let us also walk by the Spirit" (v. 25). We must see that the law, ordinances, religion, traditions, forms, rituals, regulations, mere doctrinal teachings, and the flesh all need to go. Only Christ as the life-giving Spirit mingled with our spirit must remain. Eventually, we must care for nothing but walking by the Spirit. Then we will all be marvelous Christians. Whenever we come together, we will have genuine oneness, joy, and rejoicing. To live and walk in this way are to have the proper church life.

According to the present situation in Christianity, it is often difficult to recognize Christians by their life and walk. Only after speaking with someone for a long time can we discover that he is a believer. At this point he may ask, "What church do you go to, and what are your particular practices?" This is a poor situation. Instead, if all the Christians on the earth were living and walking by the Spirit, wherever we go we would immediately recognize the brothers and sisters by their joyful praising and calling on the Lord, and we would spontaneously enjoy the church life with them in oneness.

We all must be unloaded and unburdened of the things of religion to see that the genuine and real church life is simply Christ as the life-giving Spirit living in our spirit, and we must walk by this wonderful Spirit. Then we will come to the Bible in a living way, not in the way of dead letters, and we will preach the gospel, not in a traditional way but in a fresh, instant, and living way. A visitor to our meetings once asked if the church goes to the streets to contact people. I replied to him, "Our preaching of the gospel is according to the Body of Christ." The Body is not like a machine that moves in set ways. To do the same things on certain set days is the old, traditional, religious way. Rather, the Body does many different things in a living way. Today the Body is moving in one way, and tomorrow it may move in another way. This is the practice of the genuine church life.

Because we are living, we often praise the Lord exultingly. As a result, everyone knows that we are "crazy" lovers of Jesus. However, many Christians today do not praise the Lord or speak for Him in their daily lives. Even some who claim to have the baptism of the Holy Spirit do not sing or speak for the Lord until they are in a meeting, where they are able to exercise their gifts in the way of a performance. This is not the genuine baptism of the Spirit or the proper exercise of the gifts. We need to drop all the old traditions. We do not oppose the exercise of the gifts, but we do not care for the traditional, religious, and even fleshly way of displaying them. We neither oppose nor promote any particular practice. However, some dear saints have become "addicted" to traditions, ordinances, and religion. Therefore, we need to be delivered from these things to care only for Christ, not the Christ of mere doctrines, stories, and history but the living, practical, and instant Christ. In Him we have no problems, and in Him we are one with one another. "If we live by the Spirit, let us also walk by the Spirit" (v. 25). To live and walk in this way is true freedom. Christ has set us free, and we must never again be entangled by anything else. Anything other than Christ is just an entanglement, but Christ has released us. In Him we have freedom, peace, and joy.

CHAPTER SIX

LIVING IN THE NEW CREATION AS THE ULTIMATE ISSUE OF THE BOOK OF GALATIANS

Scripture Reading: Gal. 6:1, 7-8, 12-18; 2 Cor. 5:17; Eph. 2:15; 4:24; Col. 3:10-11

AN OVERVIEW OF THE BOOK OF GALATIANS

Galatians 1 tells us how religion with its traditions is versus Christ and the church (vv. 3-4, 13-14, 15a, 16a), and chapter 2 tells us that the law with its ordinances is in opposition to Christ as our life (vv. 11-13, 19-21). Chapter 3 speaks concerning the flesh and the Spirit. Having begun by the Spirit, we should not try to be perfected by the flesh (vv. 2-3). Rather, we must remain in the Spirit and deny the flesh. Moreover, the promise of the Spirit, which we have received, is the blessing of Abraham through the gospel that was preached to him by God (vv. 8, 14). Following this, chapter 4 reveals that the flesh working together with the law produces children according to the flesh, and the Spirit working through grace produces children according to the Spirit (vv. 21-31), who are sons of God and heirs through God, inheriting all the riches of God (vv. 4-7). In order to be sons of God and heirs of God's riches, we need Christ revealed in us, Christ living in us, Christ put upon us, and Christ formed in us (v. 19). Christ, who is the Son of God, is being formed in us to make us sons of God. In principle, this means that we become the same as Christ. In ourselves we could never be the sons of God; we can only be the sons of the devil (John 8:44; 1 John 3:8, 10). In order for us to be the sons of God, we need to have Christ formed in our inner being to make us the same as He is.

A genuine believer is a son of God, but he may not always bear the image of a son of God. This is because even though he has Christ revealed in him, living in him, and put upon him, he may not have Christ adequately formed in his entire being. For this reason, Paul says to the Galatians, "My children, with whom I travail again in birth until Christ is formed in you" (4:19). Paul's intent was that the Galatians would fully become Christ. Only in this way could they be sons of God in practicality. We may illustrate this by a young man who is the son of a king and the successor to the royal throne. The young man may not yet appear to be a proper heir of the throne. This means that the kingship still needs to grow and be formed within him. Then one day, before he even ascends to the throne, everyone will be able to testify that he is already a king. Many in Christianity hold the teaching that every saved believer will enter into the coming millennium to be the kings in the kingdom. We should not believe this. Even if many were to be given the kingship outwardly, they would not have the inner growth, measure, or stature of a king. We need Christ to be formed in us until we are the same as He is in life and in nature.

Galatians 1 through 4 tells us that we need Christ revealed in us, Christ living in us, Christ put upon us, and Christ formed in us. After this, chapter 5 speaks concerning our need to walk by the Spirit (vv. 16, 25). Christ today is the all-inclusive One dwelling in our spirit. He is one with our spirit, and we are one with Him as the Spirit. Now we need to walk by the Spirit. Then chapter 6 tells us that as we walk by the Spirit, we need to restore a fallen brother in a spirit of meekness (v. 1). This is one example of our Christian service. In our service to the Lord, we must do everything in our spirit. Such a Christian life is a sowing life. Whatever we do, whatever we say, and wherever we go is a sowing. If we sow unto the Spirit and not to the flesh, we will of the Spirit reap eternal life (vv. 7-8). Then Paul concludes this Epistle by telling people that he has nothing to do with the religious world and that neither circumcision nor uncircumcision are anything. Rather, what we need is the new creation (vv. 14-15). If we walk by the Spirit and enjoy the riches of Christ in our spirit, we will spontaneously be a part of the new creation, which is the new man, the church.

In verse 17 Paul says, "Henceforth let no one trouble me." Paul did not want to be troubled with the Judaistic religion, circumcision, the keeping of the Sabbath, or any such thing. Then he continues, "I bear in my body the brands of Jesus." In the ancient times, when a man was sold as a slave, the buyer marked him with a brand to indicate his ownership over him. For Paul to bear the brands of Jesus indicated that he was the slave of Christ Jesus (Rom. 1:1). From the first day that Jesus appeared to Paul, He branded him with the "hot iron" of the cross. As a slave of Jesus, purchased by Him, Paul no longer cared for the things of the Judaistic religion. Finally, Paul closes Galatians by saying, "The grace of our Lord Jesus Christ be with your spirit, brothers. Amen" (6:18). At this point there is no religion, tradition, laws, ordinances, or the flesh; there is only Christ as the all-inclusive Spirit living in our spirit. Now we must walk and live in this spirit and sow unto the Spirit. Then we will reap eternal life, the totality of which is the new creation, the new man, the church.

RESTORING A BROTHER IN A SPIRIT OF MEEKNESS AND SOWING TO THE SPIRIT TO REAP A HARVEST OF ETERNAL LIFE

The first major item mentioned in Galatians 6 is the human spirit. Verse 1 says, "Brothers, even if a man is overtaken in some offense, you who are spiritual restore such a one in a spirit of meekness." The most important matter in restoring a fallen brother is that we do it in our spirit. It is not adequate merely to use our good heart or our mind, emotions, and will. We must restore our brother in a spirit of meekness. Our human spirit is the proper organ with which to care for the brothers.

Following this, verses 7 and 8 say, "Do not be deceived: God is not mocked; for whatever a man sows, this he will also reap. For he who sows unto his own flesh will reap corruption of the flesh, but he who sows unto the Spirit will of the Spirit reap eternal life." Paul refers to our actions, walk, and living as our sowing. Day after day and hour by hour, the things we do and the way we live are a sowing. We must be careful concerning our sowing. If we sow unto our flesh, we will reap corruption of the flesh, but if we sow unto the Spirit, we will of the Spirit reap eternal life.

As we have seen, in chapter 5 the Spirit is the One who dwells in and mingles with our regenerated spirit. This Spirit in our spirit is versus the flesh, and the flesh is versus the Spirit (vv. 16-18, 25). Following this, 6:1 speaks of a spirit of meekness, indicating that the emphasis in the latter chapter is our human spirit, which is indwelt by and mingled with the Holy Spirit. In the mingled spirit, it is our human spirit that takes the initiative. If we sow to our flesh, that is, walk according to the flesh, we will reap corruption, but if we sow to the Spirit by walking according to our mingled spirit, we will reap eternal life.

The way we talk to the brothers and sisters is an example of sowing. To speak with a brother in a fleshly way is to sow to the flesh. If we do this, we will reap corruption. Gossiping is a very corrupting factor in human society. Although speaking about others in a loose manner passes corrupting "germs" from one person to another, as fallen human beings, we are accustomed to doing this. Because of this, there is the possibility of gossiping even in the church life, which is the real social and communal life. To do this is to sow to the flesh, causing ourselves, others, and the whole church to be corrupted. It is good to communicate with other brothers and even other churches, but we must be careful not to spread deadening and corrupting germs by speaking with one another according to the flesh. We must be careful to sow only to the spirit. Then we can be assured that we will reap the eternal, divine, uncreated life as our harvest.

BEING CRUCIFIED TO THE WORLD OF CHRISTIANITY

In verse 1 of chapter 6, Paul speaks of our human spirit as the proper organ for serving the Lord by restoring a fallen brother, and in verse 8 he speaks of sowing to the mingled spirit. Following this, Paul points out that circumcision, a strong ordinance of the Judaistic religion, is merely a good show in the flesh. Verses 12 and 13 say, "As many as desire to make a good show in the flesh, these compel you to be circumcised, but only that they may not be persecuted for the cross of Christ. For neither do they that become circumcised keep the law themselves, but they desire you to be circumcised that they may boast in your flesh." In principle, all religious ordinances are shows in the flesh, such as the wearing of brightly colored robes by a choir and the singing of solos by specially talented persons. We must condemn all fleshly shows.

Then in verse 14 Paul says, "Far be it from me to boast except in the cross of our Lord Jesus Christ, through whom the world has been crucified to me and I to the world." For many centuries most Christian teachers have not understood the proper meaning of *the world* in this verse, supposing that it refers to the secular world. According to the context of Galatians, *world* refers to the religious world. Both verses 13 and 15 deal with circumcision, indicating that the "world" mentioned between these two verses is religion. Circumcision, as an ordinance of the Jewish religion, has been crucified on the cross, and we have been crucified to it. We have nothing to do with this religious world. This matches 1:4, which says that Christ "gave Himself for our sins that He might rescue us out of the present evil age." An age is a part of the world, which is the satanic system. Between us and religion is the cross. Religion as a world has been crucified to us, and we have been crucified to religion. In today's terms we may say that Christianity as a world is crucified to us, and we to the world of Christianity. I was born and raised in the world of Christianity. Even before I believed in the Lord Jesus, I contended for Christianity against Buddhism. Christianity was a true world to me. However, one day I said good-bye to that religious world. The religious world was crucified to me, and I to that world.

THE NEW CREATION BEING THE ULTIMATE ISSUE OF THE BOOK OF GALATIANS

The New Creation Having the Divine Life and Nature as Its Constitution

In 5:6 Paul says, "In Christ Jesus neither circumcision

avails anything nor uncircumcision, but faith avails, operating through love." Then again in 6:15 he says, "Neither is circumcision anything nor uncircumcision, but a new creation is what matters." The book of Galatians concludes with the new creation, which is the issue of all the things dealt with in chapters 1 through 6. The new creation is the new man in Christ, which corporately is Christ's Body, the church (Eph. 4:24; 2:15-16; Col. 3:10-11). God has two creations, the old creation and the new creation. The old creation is God's work, but it does not have God's life and nature in it. God was among His old creation, but He did not enter into it. The new creation, however, has God within it. God as the basic element of the new creation has been wrought into it. The old creation is composed of the heavens, the earth, and billions of items, including man. Strictly speaking, the new creation, does not include all these items; it is simply the church as the new man. In the future we will have the new heavens and the new earth, but even the new heavens and earth will not have the divine nature in them. They will be restored, but they will not be renewed with the divine element. Only the church has God as the basic element in it. This is signified by the golden lampstands, which are a sign of the churches and which consummate in the New Jerusalem as the city of gold (Rev. 1:12, 20; 21:18, 21). In typology gold signifies divinity. The new heaven and the new earth will not have the element of divinity, but the New Jerusalem—the ultimate expression, manifestation, and consummation of the church as the new man—will be constituted with the divine life and nature. Today every local church is a miniature of the New Jerusalem, having God Himself as its basic element. No human words can exhaust what the new creation is. Nevertheless, we are in it, and we are a part of it. We are not merely what we were created as in the old creation; we are a part of the new creation, having the divine life and nature as our constitution.

Dropping the Ordinances
to Have the New Man in Practicality

Paul says that neither circumcision avails anything nor uncircumcision. This means that to have a traditional religious practice is nothing, and to reject that practice is also nothing in itself. Likewise, to shout in the meetings is nothing in itself, and to be silent is also nothing; both to keep religious forms and to drop all the forms are nothing. Rather, a new creation is what matters. This is why we do not care for the law, religion, traditions, ordinances, or the flesh. We care only for Christ as the life-giving Spirit filling our spirit. If Christianity were to drop its ordinances, it may have very little left. The reason that Christianity maintains its ordinances is to make people appear to be living, even if they are dead (Rev. 3:1). This is to cheat people. Some claim that certain practices in Christianity, such as the clergy-laity system, choirs, and Sunday schools are necessary. These things may be necessary for Christianity, but they are not necessary for the church. Outward forms and ordinances are necessary only for the dead ones, not for the living ones.

The new creation is the new man. Ephesians 2:15 says, "Abolishing in His flesh the law of the commandments in ordinances, that He might create the two in Himself into one new man, so making peace." The Lord Jesus abolished all the ordinances in order to bring together the two peoples—the Jews and the Gentiles—to create the church as the one new man. Although the Lord slew all the ordinances and buried them in a tomb, Christianity has opened the tomb to attempt to bring them back. As a result, the unique new man that the Lord created has now been divided. Christianity is divided mainly by ordinances, such as the various methods of baptism. The New Testament teaches us that we must baptize people, but the Lord has no intention that we make baptism an ordinance. In this matter alone there are many different ordinances. To baptize by immersion is an ordinance to some, and baptizing by sprinkling is an ordinance to others. Moreover, the number of times to immerse someone, the direction in which to immerse them, and the kind of water to immerse them in are more ordinances. If we testify to someone that we are saved and that we love the Lord Jesus, he may simply ask where we were baptized, believing that baptism only according to his ordinance is able to cause people to be saved. Many divisions have been produced over this issue alone.

Methods of studying the Bible, practicing the gifts, and conducting our meetings can all become ordinances. We must never let our practices become ordinances. If a good practice becomes an ordinance, we should be the first ones to drop it. If we have the assurance that we are practicing something in the spirit, it is good to do it, but if we are not in the spirit, we should stop. Galatians 5:13 says, "You were called for freedom, brothers; only do not turn this freedom into an opportunity for the flesh, but through love serve one another." Our freedom in Christ is precious, but we should not take advantage of and abuse this freedom. When we practice something in our meetings, we must be sure that we do it in the spirit. This all depends on our daily living. Day by day and hour by hour we must be one with the dear Lord Jesus. We should always say, "Lord Jesus, I love You. I am one with You. I do not care for my desires, feelings, wishes, tendencies, intentions, likes, or dislikes. I do not care for myself. Lord Jesus, I care only for You. You are the living Spirit who lives in me, and I am one with You." If we do this, we will come to the meetings with the rich experiences of Christ, and our spirit will be strong, high, and released. Then whatever we do in the meetings will minister Christ to the members of His Body. We will not hold to laws, ordinances, religion, traditions, or regulations. We will simply have the reality of the living Jesus, which is the reality of the new creation, the new man, the church life. In this reality there are no divisions, no confusion, no Greek, no Jew, no barbarian, no Scythian, no bond man, and no free man. Rather, Christ is all and in all (Col. 3:10-11). This kind of church life is the very thing that the Lord is recovering today.

We must all ask the Lord to have mercy upon us. According to our natural birth, we are all religious. The element and disposition of religion are in our blood, but they have already been put on the cross. Christ as the all-inclusive Spirit living in our spirit is now our new source, new nature, and new life. Therefore, we must walk by the Spirit, sow to the Spirit, and enjoy all the riches of the all-inclusive Christ in our spirit. For this reason, Paul concludes Galatians by saying, "The grace of our Lord Jesus Christ be with your spirit, brothers. Amen"

(6:18). We need to digest and assimilate all the matters that we have fellowshipped in this series of messages in order to make them our living. Then we will enjoy the church life in the Lord's recovery, not merely in a doctrinal way but richly, in practicality and actuality. This depends on our faithfulness to go on with the Lord in our spirit.

ABOUT THE AUTHOR

Witness Lee was born in 1905 in northern China and raised in a Christian family. At age 19 he was fully captured for Christ and immediately consecrated himself to preach the gospel for the rest of his life. Early in his service, he met Watchman Nee, a renowned preacher, teacher, and writer. Witness Lee labored together with Watchman Nee under his direction. In 1934 Watchman Nee entrusted Witness Lee with the responsibility for his publication operation, called the Shanghai Gospel Bookroom.

Prior to the Communist takeover in 1949, Witness Lee was sent by Watchman Nee and his other co-workers to Taiwan to ensure that the things delivered to them by the Lord would not be lost. Watchman Nee instructed Witness Lee to continue the former's publishing operation abroad as the Taiwan Gospel Bookroom, which has been publicly recognized as the publisher of Watchman Nee's works outside China. Witness Lee's work in Taiwan manifested the Lord's abundant blessing. From a mere 350 believers, newly fled from the mainland, the churches in Taiwan grew to 20,000 in five years.

In 1962 Witness Lee felt led of the Lord to come to the United States, settling in California. During his 35 years of service in the U.S., he ministered in weekly meetings and weekend conferences, delivering several thousand spoken messages. Much of his speaking has since been published as over 400 titles. Many of these have been translated into over fourteen languages. He gave his last public conference in February 1997 at the age of 91.

He leaves behind a prolific presentation of the truth in the Bible. His major work, *Life-study of the Bible,* comprises over 25,000 pages of commentary on every book of the Bible from the perspective of the believers' enjoyment and experience of God's divine life in Christ through the Holy Spirit. Witness Lee was the chief editor of a new translation of the New Testament into Chinese called the Recovery Version and directed the translation of the same into English. The Recovery Version also appears in a number of other languages. He provided an extensive body of footnotes, outlines, and spiritual cross references. A radio broadcast of his messages can be heard on Christian radio stations in the United States. In 1965 Witness Lee founded Living Stream Ministry, a non-profit corporation, located in Anaheim, California, which officially presents his and Watchman Nee's ministry.

Witness Lee's ministry emphasizes the experience of Christ as life and the practical oneness of the believers as the Body of Christ. Stressing the importance of attending to both these matters, he led the churches under his care to grow in Christian life and function. He was unbending in his conviction that God's goal is not narrow sectarianism but the Body of Christ. In time, believers began to meet simply as the church in their localities in response to this conviction. In recent years a number of new churches have been raised up in Russia and in many eastern European countries.

OTHER BOOKS PUBLISHED BY
Living Stream Ministry

Titles by Witness Lee:

Abraham—Called by God	978-0-7363-0359-0
The Experience of Life	978-0-87083-417-2
The Knowledge of Life	978-0-87083-419-6
The Tree of Life	978-0-87083-300-7
The Economy of God	978-0-87083-415-8
The Divine Economy	978-0-87083-268-0
God's New Testament Economy	978-0-87083-199-7
The World Situation and God's Move	978-0-87083-092-1
Christ vs. Religion	978-0-87083-010-5
The All-inclusive Christ	978-0-87083-020-4
Gospel Outlines	978-0-87083-039-6
Character	978-0-87083-322-9
The Secret of Experiencing Christ	978-0-87083-227-7
The Life and Way for the Practice of the Church Life	978-0-87083-785-2
The Basic Revelation in the Holy Scriptures	978-0-87083-105-8
The Crucial Revelation of Life in the Scriptures	978-0-87083-372-4
The Spirit with Our Spirit	978-0-87083-798-2
Christ as the Reality	978-0-87083-047-1
The Central Line of the Divine Revelation	978-0-87083-960-3
The Full Knowledge of the Word of God	978-0-87083-289-5
Watchman Nee—A Seer of the Divine Revelation ...	978-0-87083-625-1

Titles by Watchman Nee:

How to Study the Bible	978-0-7363-0407-8
God's Overcomers	978-0-7363-0433-7
The New Covenant	978-0-7363-0088-9
The Spiritual Man • 3 volumes	978-0-7363-0269-2
Authority and Submission	978-0-7363-0185-5
The Overcoming Life	978-1-57593-817-2
The Glorious Church	978-0-87083-745-6
The Prayer Ministry of the Church	978-0-87083-860-6
The Breaking of the Outer Man and the Release ...	978-1-57593-955-1
The Mystery of Christ	978-1-57593-954-4
The God of Abraham, Isaac, and Jacob	978-0-87083-932-0
The Song of Songs	978-0-87083-872-9
The Gospel of God • 2 volumes	978-1-57593-953-7
The Normal Christian Church Life	978-0-87083-027-3
The Character of the Lord's Worker	978-1-57593-322-1
The Normal Christian Faith	978-0-87083-748-7
Watchman Nee's Testimony	978-0-87083-051-8

Available at
Christian bookstores, or contact Living Stream Ministry
2431 W. La Palma Ave. • Anaheim, CA 92801
1-800-549-5164 • www.livingstream.com